Pebble® Plus

How to Make a
Bouncing Egg

Hands-On
SCIENCE
FUN

by Jennifer L. Marks

Consulting Editor: Gail Saunders-Smith, PhD

Consultant: Ronald Browne, PhD
Department of Elementary & Early Childhood Education
Minnesota State University, Mankato

CAPSTONE PRESS
a capstone imprint

Pebble Plus is published by Capstone Press,
151 Good Counsel Drive, P.O. Box 669, Mankato, Minnesota 56002.
www.capstonepub.com

Books published by Capstone Press are manufactured with paper
containing at least 10 percent post-consumer waste.

Library of Congress Cataloging-in-Publication Data
Marks, Jennifer, 1979–
  How to make a bouncing egg / by Jennifer L. Marks.
     p. cm.—(Pebble plus. Hands-on science fun)
  Summary: "Simple text and full-color photos instruct readers how to make a bouncing egg and explain the science
behind the activity"—Provided by publisher.
  Includes bibliographical references and index.
  ISBN 978-1-4296-5291-9 (library binding)
  ISBN 978-1-4296-6214-7 (paperback)
  1. Chemistry—Experiments—Juvenile literature. 2. Calcium carbonate—Solubility—Juvenile literature. 3. Eggs—
Experiments—Juvenile literature. 4. Science—Study and teaching—Activity programs—Juvenile literature. 5.
Science—Study and teaching (Primary)—Activity programs—Juvenile literature. I. Title. II. Series.
  QD43.M327 2011
  507.8—dc22   2010024911

Editorial Credits
Erika L. Shores, editor; Gene Bentdahl, designer; Sarah Schuette, photo shoot direction; Marcy Morin, scheduler;
     Laura Manthe, production specialist

Photo Credits
Capstone Studio/Karon Dubke, all

Note to Parents and Teachers

The Hands-On Science Fun series supports national science standards related to physical
science. This book describes and illustrates how to make a bouncing egg. The images support
early readers in understanding the text. The repetition of words and phrases helps early readers
learn new words. This book also introduces early readers to subject-specific vocabulary words,
which are defined in the Glossary section. Early readers may need assistance to read some
words and to use the Table of Contents, Glossary, Read More, Internet Sites, and Index sections
of the book.

Printed in the United States of America in North Mankato, Minnesota.
092010
005933CGS11

Table of Contents

Safety Note:
Please ask an adult for help in making your bouncing egg.

Getting Started

Splat! Have you ever dropped
an egg? The shell cracks.
The egg white and slimy yolk
run everywhere!
But not if it's a bouncing egg.

Here's what you need:

1 raw egg

medium bowl
or glass

white vinegar

5

Making a Bouncing Egg

Take one raw egg

from an egg carton.

Gently place the egg inside

a medium bowl or glass.

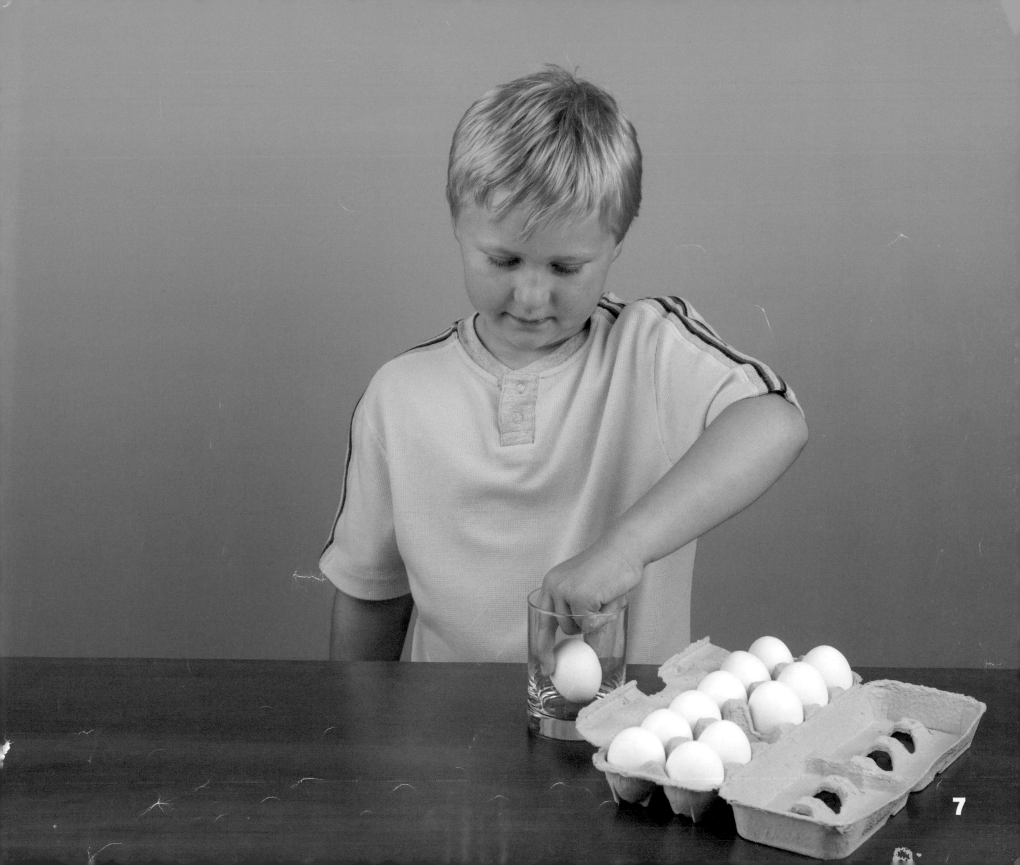

Slowly pour white vinegar

into the bowl or glass.

Add enough vinegar

to completely cover the egg.

Now, let the egg soak.

Put the soaking egg

somewhere it won't be bothered.

Leave the egg in the vinegar

for at least three days.

Look at the egg every day

to see how it changes.

Day 1

Day 2

Day 3

11

After three days, take the egg

out of the container.

What does it feel like?

Is it soft and rubbery?

13

Hold the egg a few inches
above a smooth, hard surface.
When you let go of the egg,
it won't break. It will bounce!

How Does It Work?

Eggshells are made from calcium.

The acid in vinegar

breaks down calcium.

After a few days, the vinegar

dissolves the shell.

Vinegar changes the inside of an egg too. The egg's membrane absorbs vinegar and thickens. The strong membrane lets the egg bounce.

Bouncing eggs do not crack

easily like normal eggs.

But don't drop the bouncing egg

from too high or—splat!

The egg is still breakable.

Glossary

absorb—to soak up

acid—a strong liquid; the acetic acid in vinegar breaks down calcium carbonate in eggshells

calcium—a soft, silver-white mineral

dissolve—to break into tiny pieces when mixed with a liquid

membrane—a very thin layer that separates the inside of an egg from its hard outer shell

rubbery—strong and able to stretch

shell—the hard outer covering around an egg

soak—to leave something in a liquid

yolk—the yellow part of an egg

Read More

Sandvold, Lynnette Brent. *Time for Kids Super Science Book*. New York: Time for Kids Books, 2009.

VanCleave, Janice. *Janice VanCleave's Big Book of Play and Find Out Science Projects*. New York: Jossey-Bass, 2007.

Internet Sites

FactHound offers a safe, fun way to find Internet sites related to this book. All of the sites on FactHound have been researched by our staff.

Here's all you do:

Visit *www.facthound.com*

Type in this code: 9781429652919

 Check out projects, games and lots more at **www.capstonekids.com**

Index

Word Count: 208

Grade: 1

Early-Intervention Level: 18